SCRUM

Mastering Agile Project Management
for Exceptional Results
(2023 Guide for Beginners)

Whitney Soto

Contents

Chapter 1: Basics of scrum

Scrum is a process framework that enables team members to deal with a broad range of complicated and ever-changing challenges in a creative manner while staying productive and producing results.

Products that meet or surpass expectations. While Scrum is relatively lightweight and simple to grasp at first, it can also be extremely complex and take years to master.

Jeff Sutherland and Ken Schwaber established it in the early 1990s for use in software development, but it has now been adopted in a broad range of other sectors as well. Scrum's main strength is that it makes determining the overall effectiveness of work procedures and product management relatively simple, while also making it simpler to deal with the challenges that arise while seeking to constantly improve the working environment, team, and product.

The Scrum framework is made up of numerous Scrum Teams, as well as the rules, artifacts, events, and responsibilities that go with them. Each of these components therefore serves a distinct function, with the final result being critical to the Scrum framework's continuous use and overall success. Meanwhile, Scrum rules are what bind the interactions between the main relationships, artifacts, events, and roles that allow the Scrum framework to function as efficiently as possible.

Scrum employs

While Scrum was initially used to develop products, it has been used in a wide range of industries for nearly 30 years to do things like:

Determine the viability of markets, goods, and technology.

Identify items that may be improved or refined.

Iterating and creating new product versions or enhancements as rapidly as possible

Maintain current operating environments while also developing new ones, including

cloud environments.

Existing items should be renewed and maintained.

Scrum has been widely employed in the development of hardware, software, embedded software, and the like because of its quick iteration process. It has also been utilized for nearly everything else, including the development of autonomous vehicles, governments, schools, marketing tactics, and several other organizational functions.

Scrum was developed about 30 years ago, and as the interconnections between environmental, market, and technical complications have expanded, it has shown its effectiveness in dealing with life's complexities on a daily basis. It has also shown particular effectiveness at enhancing procedures involving incremental and iterative knowledge transfers.

Scrum is really about small teams of individuals working together as efficiently as possible. These teams are incredibly adaptable and versatile, and these qualities can be maintained regardless of how many teams are functioning simultaneously. These teams may then interact and communicate using a combination of tailored development architectures and sophisticated release environments. When discussing Scrum, the words development and develop refer to any type of complex work that is taking place.

The Fundamentals of Scrum Theory

Scrum's foundations may be found in empirical process control theory, which is part of the philosophy of empiricism. The primary premise behind empiricism is that knowledge is obtained most efficiently through experience and making the best choice feasible at the time with the facts available. Scrum makes use of this concept by using an incremental and iterative approach to risk management and enhancing the predictability of the intended output.

When using the empirical process, three pillars are at work: adaptation, inspection, and transparency.

Transparency: Transparency is essential because it is critical that individuals responsible for the result of a particular process have a clear picture of how it is progressing at each stage along the way.

Furthermore, transparency is essential to ensure that anyone else who needs to see what is going on can do so. The eventual aim is for all spectators to have a broad knowledge of whatever they are witnessing.

One area where this is true is when it comes to establishing a consistent language throughout the process that can be shared by everyone involved. For example, people developing the product and those analyzing the results must share the same concept of when the project is finished.

Scrum users are typically needed to inspect Scrum items as they advance toward a goal in order to identify any deviations that may be detrimental to that objective. These inspections should not be conducted so often that they interfere with the job being done; instead, they are most effective when performed methodically by personnel who are adept at examining this phase of work.

Adaptation: When an inspector discovers that any component or aspect of the process is diverging more than is allowed or that the resultant product may eventually be undesirable, the process must be altered as soon as feasible to prevent more deviation. When adaptation is necessary, many particular activities occur as part of the Scrum process, including the Sprint Retrospective, Daily Scrum, Sprint Review, and Sprint Planning.

To guarantee that the Scrum pillars perform as efficiently as possible while also developing trust among the group as a whole, the whole Scrum team must live by the principles of respect, openness, focus, bravery, and commitment. As they work with various Scrum artifacts, roles, and events, Scrum team members explore and learn to embody these values. Ultimately, using Scrum effectively demands that team members become more adaptable at embodying these particular ideals over time. Similarly, the team must feel compelled to personally commit to attaining the Scrum team's objectives.

It is critical that the Scrum team feels sufficiently supported to have the guts to always do the right thing on a project, no matter how tough it may seem at the moment. If the Scrum Team and its many sorts of stakeholders can all agree to be transparent about the work that is being done and the issues that are being encountered, mutual respect will thrive, and everyone will be able to concentrate on the work of each sprint and the team's overall objectives.

Members of the group

The Scrum team consists of the Scrum Master, the Development Team, and the Product Owner. Scrum teams are cross-functional and self-organizing, which means that each team member is accountable for deciding how to do their task most efficiently rather than being guided one way or another by one person or, worse, someone outside the team altogether. A team is termed cross-functional if it comprises numerous people who can complete each component of the objective, essentially ensuring that the team never needs to depend on anybody else to get the work done. Scrum team models were created to maximize flexibility, productivity, and innovation.

The Scrum team works iteratively, which means they produce things progressively with the purpose of providing as many chances for feedback as feasible. Each new version is as full as feasible, so that, at the very least, a usable version of the project is always accessible.

Product creator: The product owner is the team member responsible for ensuring that the development team's work is utilized to its full potential. What this entails will vary greatly depending on the project's industry and the particular product owner. One thing that will never change is that the product owner is the sole person in charge of managing any product backlog. These tasks can be delegated to the development team, but the product owner is still responsible for them. These duties include the following:

Clearly and concisely expressing available items in the product backlog

Placing these objects to ensure that they are linked in the best manner to meet tasks

and goals

Work to make the backlog obvious to everyone so that the next job to be completed

is evident.

It is critical that the product owner be a single person rather than a group of

people; however, they may work toward shared objectives if they desire. Regardless, if

the priority of a specific item is to change, the product owner must approve the change.

To ensure the product owner's eventual success, it is critical that it be made clear that the whole company respects their judgments. Similarly, it must be clear that no one else has the authority to alter what the development team is working on or their current requirements.

Team in Charge of Development: The Development Team is made up of folks who perform the real labor of developing something that can be designated as "done." This marks the conclusion of the current sprint since it is necessary to proceed to the Sprint Review phase of the procedure. The increment may only be created by members of this team.

The development team should be formed in such a manner that its members feel empowered to manage their own work and arrange themselves as they see appropriate. The resultant synergy helps to improve their overall efficacy and efficiency. The following criteria are shared by effective development teams:

They have the authority to convert backlog items into possibly usable increments as

they see fit.

Members of the Development Team are Development Team members

There is no other categorization in the area.

Similarly, there are no recognized sub-teams inside the development team

They may convene whenever they like.

All responsibility is shared by the entire team.

The development team should be small enough to pivot as required but big enough to perform a sufficient amount of work within each sprint. In general, if your development team does not include at least three people, you will notice less interaction and, hence, lesser productivity increases. Similarly, smaller teams are more likely to be constrained by the skills they have or do not have, eventually reaching a point where they cannot actively improve the increment in question without going outside the team.

However, anything more than ten people can make it difficult to effectively coordinate everyone, resulting in decreased gains. Furthermore, they can add so many moving parts to the puzzle that the empirical process begins to fail. The Scrum Master and Product Owner are not featured in this category unless they are also actively working on the Sprint Backlog.

Chapter 2: The sprint

wwhile Scrum's organizational style is relatively freeform, it still employs a number of events to help add some regularity to the process and reduce the need for extraneous events that are not required.

Scrum has explicitly dictated Scrum events are by definition time-boxed, which implies they have a maximum potential duration. The sprint is the main event in the Scrum process since it includes all of the other events that may occur during the production of a single iteration of a product. After a sprint begins, its duration is fixed and cannot be changed, whether to lengthen or shorten it.

The Sprint events may all be seen as independent opportunities to adjust or check anything. These events are specifically intended to allow for the amount of deep examination required for real transparency in crucial operations. As a result, if any of these events are missed or skipped for any reason, the Scrum team's ability to inspect and adapt the process is weakened, resulting in an overall reduced level of transparency that will harm not only the current sprint but all subsequent sprints based on the incomplete data.

The Sprint

The sprint is a time-box of no more than a month in which the Scrum team produces a finished product that is possibly releasable but definitely usable in some manner, known internally as an increment. Throughout the development of the product, sprints should all be the same length. As soon as the previous sprint concludes, a new one should begin.

Sprint planning, development work, daily scrums, and the sprint retrospective will all be part of each sprint.

During each sprint, it is critical that no changes to the scope of the product or increment are made that would make it impossible to meet the current sprint goal. Similarly, quality targets cannot be reduced throughout the sprint, but the scope may be renegotiated or clarified if the product owner and development team determine that prior forecasts were erroneous.

Each sprint is a kind of project with a maximum time horizon of one month. Sprints, like projects, are meant to achieve something particular, which means that each sprint will naturally have a purpose in terms of what will be developed, what the design will look like, and a broad, flexible strategy that will put the development team on the correct track. It will also clearly specify the scope of the work to be done and the consequent increment.

It is critical to ensure that the sprint's scope does not become so extensive that you are tempted to extend its length. If the time horizon for a single sprint becomes too lengthy, the scope is likely to alter too much, and the total complexity and risk may turn it into something altogether different. Sprints are beneficial because they are predictable, and they are predictable because they allow for adaptation and examination as well as progress toward the objective in a fair amount of time. Limiting the Sprint duration makes it easy to monitor expenditures on a monthly basis.

Sprint cancellation: While a Sprint cannot be prolonged, it may be terminated before the Sprint time box is naturally completed. However, only the product owner has the authority to do so, though they may listen to anyone else involved in the matter, including the shareholders, the scrum master, and the development team.

In general, the only meaningful reason to terminate a sprint after it has begun is if the sprint goal becomes outdated. This might happen if the company's aims change throughout the Sprint or if the technology or market circumstances change in general.

In general, a sprint should be performed only if it no longer makes sense under the present conditions. This should be unusual owing to the short period of time that a sprint is active for, particularly when the duration is so brief.

If a Sprint is canceled, the first thing that should be done is to review any product backlog items that have been generated. If any of the increments are usable or releasable, the product owner will accept them, while the remaining items are returned to the backlog with a new completion estimate. Any work that is not immediately usable has a short shelf life and must be re-estimated if it is to be used properly.

It is critical to remember that if a Sprint contract is canceled, all of its used resources are lost due to what is not reusable.

Furthermore, additional resources will be required before anything useful is generated, as the Scrum team must return to square one in order to resume work. As a result, canceling a sprint may be highly stressful for a team and should be avoided if at all feasible.

Sprint Preparation: Any work that will be generated during the sprint should first be discussed during the Sprint Planning phase. This strategy should be developed collaboratively with input from the whole Scrum team. Sprint planning should be limited to no more than eight hours per month, with shorter sprints requiring shorter planning periods. The Scrum Master is in charge of ensuring that all events occur on schedule and that everyone in attendance is on the same page in terms of intended outcomes. The scrum master should also be responsible for keeping everyone else working within the time constraints.

A good sprint planning session should address numerous questions, beginning with a clear estimate of what can be provided from the increment that the sprint will create and how the work that is necessary will be performed. The development team is in charge of choosing what sorts of features will be included in the forthcoming sprint's next increment. Meanwhile, the product owner is responsible for discussing the objective of the current sprint goal and noting the items in the backlog that they feel would assist in fulfilling it and therefore be most successful in helping everyone achieve their goals. Meanwhile, the entire Scrum team should work together to understand the work that the sprint is doing.

The true input for this discussion should include the development team's previous project experience, their capability, the most recent increment of the product, and the available product backlog. The development team will choose the number of items from the backlog for this sprint since they are the only ones who can reliably predict what they will achieve during the sprint.

During this time, the Scrum team as a whole sets the goal for the next sprint. This goal should be the primary aim that will be completed during the sprint based on the items picked from the backlog, and it should act as a direction for the development team as they develop the next increment.

When it comes to establishing how the work in question will be accomplished, the development team does so once the sprint goal has been developed and the next round of backlog items has been picked. When it comes to selecting how to best incorporate the specified feature into the next increment, the development team has total control. This job will naturally require differing degrees of effort and labor from smaller groups of varying sizes within the development team.

While this outline does not have to be exact, it should be formal enough to determine the scope of what can be completed during the next sprint. Furthermore, this meeting should break down exactly what needs to be done for Sprint's early days, generally in units of a single day. This plan should then be submitted to the product owner, who may be required to clarify details about backlog items and propose trade-offs if the development team has too little or too much to complete during the next sprint. Other team members or stakeholders may also be invited to this segment of the meeting if the development team gives the go-ahead.

By the end of the sprint's planning phase, the development team should be able to explain in detail how the work will be completed during the sprint to meet the target goals in question. If there is any doubt about this fact, it will be resolved here since the Sprint will then move into high gear.

Sprint Objective: The Sprint Goal's guiding principle is that it gives unambiguous advice to the Development Team when it comes to delivering the best increment possible. A good sprint target is one that allows the development team some leeway in terms of the functionality that is eventually developed within the sprint. Any backlog items picked should all aim to deliver on a single piece of the product's role, which is frequently mirrored in the Sprint target as well. It may also be any other form of coherence that keeps the development team working toward a single objective rather than splintering into multiple smaller, more personal goals.

While the development team is in the midst of a sprint, it should keep the sprint goal and what is required to see it through to completion in mind. If the work takes an unexpected turn during the sprint, it is the development team's responsibility to speak with the product owner to ensure that the sprint can continue successfully.

Scrum on a daily basis: The Daily Scrum is a 15-minute event with its own time box for the Development Team to discuss what they will be working on between now and the next Daily Scrum.

This will allow the team to be optimized as efficiently as possible for the next work while also giving a clear route for everyone to follow in order to keep everyone working towards the same goal. If at all feasible, the daily scrum should be conducted at the same time every day in order for it to be the focal point of the development team's workday.

Daily scrums are critical for guaranteeing open communication among the development team, frequently to the point of eliminating the need for additional meetings completely, organically enhancing productivity. They also allow the whole team to be informed of any obstructions to the sprint as soon as possible. Their daily nature also ensures that the team can make decisions quickly while also expanding their knowledge. As such, it is a critical component in the Sprint's capacity to improve via adaptation and examination.

The development team should utilize the daily scrum to review the work that has already been accomplished toward the sprint goal as well as what will be done next. The daily scrum is very beneficial because it provides a forum for the whole team to address concerns that may prevent the sprint from being finished on time. When the whole team is aware of the situation, it becomes considerably more manageable and will take much less time than it would otherwise. It also allows the team to rearrange as required to ensure top efficiency is maintained and validated each and every day.

The meeting's framework should be as flexible as the development team itself, and the most essential thing is that the final product is useful to people who use it. Some development teams begin each meeting with a set of questions concerning the present and future condition of the increment, while others are more conversation-driven. Again, the format chosen by your development team isn't as significant as the fact that it works for them.

In this case, the Scrum Master's duty is to guarantee that the development team conducts their meeting without attempting to lead the daily scrum itself. It is also the scrum master's responsibility to guarantee that the daily scrum does not exceed its time limit. Finally, because this is an internal development team meeting, the scrum master should work to ensure that other team members do not disrupt the meeting.

Chapter 3: Looking Back on a Sprint and Planning for the Future

Sprint Review: The Sprint Review is conducted at the end of each Sprint to allow the whole Scrum Team and any relevant stakeholders to look at the new increment together for the next Sprint.

to determine what adjustments, if any, should be made to the new product backlog. Throughout the sprint review process, the team should discuss how the entire sprint went and what can be done in the future to further optimize value.

Nonetheless, this is not a status meeting; rather, the presentation of the increment serves as a means of fostering collaboration and eliciting quality feedback. If the sprint lasts a full month, the meeting should last no more than four hours. The Scrum Master is responsible for ensuring that this event occurs and that everyone involved understands its objective. They should also be responsible for limiting the meeting to an acceptable duration relative to the sprint.

Every Sprint Review should comprise a number of components, beginning with attendance; the review should include the Scrum Master, the Product Owner, the Development Team, and other stakeholders the Product Owner thinks appropriate. Before everything is said and done, the product owner should discuss what items have been checked off the product backlog with this iteration and what still needs to be completed.

The development team should then share everything that went well throughout the sprint, as well as the difficulties they encountered and how they overcame them. They will also show off anything new that the iteration can accomplish as a consequence of the sprint and answer any questions from the rest of the team concerning this particular increment.

Based on the current progress, the product owner should next describe the current condition of the product backlog as well as the revised delivery date for the final product. The whole group should then deliberate on what to do next so that the Sprint Review gives relevant feedback for the next phase of planning. This should also involve a broad analysis of how the marketplace or target audience for the product may have changed over the previous sprint and if anything else needs to change as a result.

Finally, the entire team should go over the new information about the product as a whole, as well as the current increment and what the next increment will look like if everything goes as planned. Any additional features are then added to the product backlog when they become available.

Sprint evaluation: The Sprint Retrospective is the team's last chance to check in with one another and verify that there is a plan in place to implement any adjustments that need to be made prior to the start of the following Sprint. Assuming your sprint was one month long, this meeting should not last more than three hours. The Scrum Master should be in charge of keeping everyone on track throughout the meeting and maintaining it within a realistic schedule. At the same time, the Scrum Master must participate as a peer in this meeting to ensure they have the appropriate amount of responsibility for the Scrum process as a whole.

The Sprint Retrospective is intended to help the team assess how successful the previous Sprint was in terms of tools utilized, procedures optimized, connections developed, and individuals engaged. This should include an examination of what went well as well as what went wrong in order to ensure that when the team produces an improvement plan for the following sprint, it appropriately covers the breadth of what needs to be done.

During this time, the Scrum Master should do everything possible to ensure that the Scrum Team improves while also keeping everyone tied to the Scrum process framework, with the end goal of making the process not only effective but also enjoyable. For each retrospective, the team should come up with new ways to improve product quality by improving work processes and possibly changing the definition of finished for the next sprint. Assuming, of course, that these adjustments do not contradict organizational or product standards.

The whole team should have a clear sense of the enhancements that will be made for the subsequent sprint at the conclusion of each retrospective. The adaptation element of the process is responsible for ensuring that these changes are implemented. While various types of improvements should be implemented as they are discovered throughout the Sprint, the Sprint

Retrospective provides an opportunity to focus on both adaptation and inspection in a more formal and focused context.

chapter 4: Scrum Artifiacts

A Scrum artifact is anything that reflects labor or value and allows for transparency, examination, and adaptation. Scrum artifacts are all particularly intended to increase the openness of important information to ensure that everyone understands every element of the current sprint or increment.

Backlog of products: The product backlog is an organized list of everything that will eventually be included in the product. This document will serve as the only source of requirements for any future updates to the product. The product owner will be ultimately accountable for the product's backlog, including ordering, evaluating availability, and creating content.

Regardless of how much effort is put into the product backlog at the start of the project, it will always be a living document, which means it will never be completely finished. In reality, the early stages of its development are critical since they establish the most clearly defined needs as well as those that are most vital when it comes to having a functional product up and running. The product backlog develops from there, as do the purposes and settings in which it will be employed.

The product backlog should eventually comprise all of the repairs, additions, requirements, functionalities, and features that the product will have in subsequent versions. Items in the backlog should all have well-defined features such as value, estimate, and order. These items usually contain a form of test description intended to identify whether they are complete and completely incorporated into the next increment.

As a program gains popularity and value among users and the marketplace as a whole, it generates additional feedback, and the product backlog becomes much more well-defined and extensive. These needs are always changing, which is why it is critical that the backlog be regarded as a live document.

It makes no difference how many distinct Scrum teams collaborate on a product; they should all be working from the same product backlog. The practice of adding more information and cost-benefit analysis estimates to existing product backlog items is known as refining the product backlog. This phase necessitates extra modification and evaluation of the items currently on the list, and the development team is largely responsible for choosing when this process occurs. A decent rule of thumb is that this should not exceed 10% of the development team's time. The product owner may also, at their option, change the backlog and any of its items at any moment.

In general, the higher an item is in the product backlog, the better specified it is. As a result of the improved clarity provided by all of the new features, estimations become more accurate. Backlog items that will be addressed next should be so polished that they can easily fit into the time box of the next Sprint since they are so well-defined, which means they will be regarded as ready for selection when the time comes to design the next Sprint.

In these cases, the development team is in charge of all estimations; however, the product owner does have some power as well. In this situation, the product owner will assist by making it obvious what trade-offs are possible and addressing any questions the development team may have.

Progress monitoring: The overall amount of work left should be simply tallied up during each sprint. The product owner is responsible for monitoring progress toward the end objective and updating this progress report after each sprint review. The product owner then compares the amount of work left at prior sprint reviews to the current review to confirm that everything is still on track.

The conclusions reached should subsequently be communicated with the whole team.

When it comes to anticipating progress, there are several techniques available, such as cumulative flows, burn-ups, and burn-downs. However, none of this can ever replace the raw importance of pure empiricism, especially in complex environments where the outcome is far from certain.

Sprint backlog: The Sprint backlog is both the product backlog for a single Sprint and a location for fulfilling needs within the scope of the next Sprint. It may also be seen as a prediction for the development team to begin thinking about what needs to be done in order to deliver the next increment as efficiently as possible.

The sprint backlog is useful because it makes apparent all of the work that the development team believes is required to fulfill the current sprint target. It should also contain at least one key improvement as specified by the most recent Sprint Retrospective meeting to keep the continuous improvement going. The sprint backlog should be detailed enough that any modifications made to it during the daily scrum are readily described.

When new work is required, the development team can directly add it to the Sprint backlog. When the work is finished, the estimate for any remaining work should also be updated. If certain aspects of the plan are finally reduced for any reason, they may be simply removed. During the sprint, the development team is solely responsible for changing the sprint backlog. As such, it provides a real-time, exceptionally accurate view of the work the team is presently working on and will accomplish by the end of the sprint.

Monitoring the Sprint's Progress: The entire amount of work remaining in the Sprint should be monitored in real time and summarized in a format that is readily accessible to everyone on the team. The development team should be in charge of maintaining this work total and updating it with each daily scrum to ensure that the whole scrum team is aware of the likelihood that the current target will be met during the current sprint.

Increment: The increment may be thought of as the sum of all the additional value created by the backlog items completed during the sprint, added to the value of all preceding sprints. An increment is a body of inspectable, finished work that supports both the sprint goal and the final product goal that the Scrum Team is working towards.

Chapter 5: Scrums Master as Servant Leader

Responsibilities of a Servant-Leader

A ScrumMaster is a servant-leader in the sense that it is their objective to enable the requirements of all team members as well as whomever the team serves (usually the client). They should try to create outcomes that are consistent with the Scrum Team's goals as well as the wider organization's business objectives, principles, and values.

ScrumMaster duties may include the following:

- Setting up a Scrum framework for the benefit of the team, not to command or micromanage
- giving the development team the tools they need to properly manage themselves Conflict resolution involves ensuring that every dispute is seen as a healthy exchange of ideas.
- Ensuring that every member of the team is fully conversant with the Scrum framework.
- Stepping in to manage anything that may prevent the Scrum Team from meeting the objectives of their current sprint doing everything necessary to eliminate any impediments that may arise during a sprint ensuring that everyone on both sides of the team is as open as possible.

- Helping the team in any manner that will lead to them becoming better versions of themselves
- creating a team culture that is collaborative, helpful, and compassionate keeping the team challenged and moving away from mediocrity Ensure team members' development, progress, and pleasure.

The scrum master is the scrum team's servant leader. To inspire servant leadership conduct, the Scrum Master Job is intentionally devoid of organizational authority and control. The Scrum Master is neither a boss nor an alternative title for team management.

Because there is no organizational power, the scrum master can establish psychological safety within the team. As a result, team members are empowered and may self-organize. If the scrum master has organizational influence, the odds of creating a safe atmosphere are reduced.

A Servant-leader the scrum master fosters a culture in which individuals may participate and thrive. An atmosphere in which individuals feel cared for and free to express themselves. An atmosphere in which they have the authority to make the appropriate judgments.

The scrum master is the scrum team's leader.

Who is the Scrum Master's client? The Scrum Master assists the development team, the product owner, and the organization in their efforts to implement and reap the advantages of Scrum.

A scrum master helps the scrum team achieve high performance. As a result, it can quickly adjust to changing client demands and address customer difficulties. For Scrum Masters who also happen to have organizational power—meaning accountability for product delivery, team members reporting to you, budgetary choices, performance evaluations, and so on—watch your actions carefully.

The following questions should be answered by a skilled servant-leader Scrum Master:

Will my coworkers and team members say that I serve them if asked?

Whose agenda am I advancing? Is it theirs or mine?

Is it possible for me to defend my role as a servant-leader scrum master? How does the servant-leadership style of the Scrum Master interact with conventional managers? For typical managers, the contradictory style of servant leadership is difficult to implement. Most managers are at ease with the leadership component but not with the servant part.

Serving and caring: You have no power in the company as a Scrum Master. You have influence because of your Scrum subject matter knowledge and because you have the passion to serve and care for your team.

As a servant leader, you strive to empower team members and include them in decision-making. Your attitude is one of service and concern. It promotes team member development while also increasing organizational care and quality of life.

Is your focus on servicing your team members for their benefit rather than the benefit of the organization? If so, you are a very successful scrum master.

Empowering and Assisting: The Scrum Master must be concerned with the activities of all stakeholders. Stakeholders broadly encompass society, communities, corporate partners, and workers, particularly the least fortunate among them.

Servant-Leader Scrum Masters think that team members have inherent worth beyond their job obligations.

These scrum masters are strongly devoted to the growth and development of every scrum team member. Individuals must learn to nurture both the professional and personal growth of team members while serving as Scrum Masters.

Agenda of the Serving Team: As a servant leader, a Scrum Master leverages his competencies and skills to assist the team in developing their agenda.

The Scrum Master supports the agenda of the team, not their own.

The Scrum Master does not give the team any orders or mandates. A servant-master scrum master, on the other hand, believes in change by invitation. They invite the team to decide on the objectives and direction. They encourage team members to opt in and participate while leaving the door open for anyone to opt out.

It is critical to note that if a scrum master simultaneously has typical manager responsibilities such as delivering a release or managing team members, they will not be able to properly serve the team's agenda. Such a person will almost always end up forcing people to follow their direction and goal.

There is also a limit to fulfilling the agenda of the team. For example, if a product owner's agenda is to complete a particular number of features by the conclusion of the current sprint, the team plainly perceives it as impractical.

Though you want the product owner to succeed, it is your responsibility to protect the development team from the product owner's excessive pressure. Scrum Masters often cave in to pressure and enable the PO to overburden the development team.

What do you believe happened when the development team was expected to produce more than they could physically deliver?

a) A product with flaws and low quality; **b)** Stressed and overworked team members as a result of having to work additional evenings and weekends; **c)** Technical debt accumulation

Can you say that the team's agenda was served in any of the scenarios?

Relationship Development: Establishing and sustaining long-term connections with all stakeholders, as well as keeping team members in mind, allows them to reach their full potential. Building relationships with your team members will be easy if you are sincerely serving, caring for, and assisting them in their growth. To create long-term relationships, you must abandon short-term approaches and gains and wait for things to settle.

Healthy team relationships foster synergy among team members and improve team performance and development. Is your focus on long-term, healthy relationships? If so, you're on the right track.

Being Humility: The Scrum Master, like any successful leader, maintains humility and engages in frequent self-reflection. In contrast to a typical leader's pride, servant leaders demonstrate humility in their actions. Servant leaders do not think less of themselves; they just think less of themselves.

They have a high level of self-assurance but a low level of situational confidence. When confronted with an issue, their most probable reaction is: "I have the intellect to solve all the problems, but I don't have all the answers, and for that, I need other people's brains."

In today's environment, when there is so much information and so many tools, it is critical to recognize that one person cannot know everything and that everyone needs or will require the assistance of his or her team members at some point. A servant leader will not take pleasure in moments of achievement but will accept mistakes when they occur.

Emotional recovery: Your personnel are always undergoing change. There is insecurity and failure. Some of your team members may have bruises. Many of them may experience emotional upheaval.

Are you able to help them emotionally? Offer your assistance?

According to the team development model, the team goes through four stages: forming, norming, storming, and performing. As a Scrum Master, are you supporting your team as it goes through the Forming, Norming, and Storming phases of team development? As a servant leader, whatever emotional healing and support you provide may go a long way toward creating a team culture of trust and compassion.

Being empathic entails profoundly connecting with the feelings of another person without judgment or criticism. It is a necessary trait of servant leaders. Listening is the first step toward empathy. Being really present in the moment with someone and listening with your full self helps in understanding the other person's predicament. The goal here is to slow down and listen with the idea of understanding the meaning behind the words and the significance of what is felt and what is not spoken. Empathy binds two individuals together at the heart. Connecting with someone via the heart is much more powerful than connecting through the head.

Being aware of and caring about the emotions of others is the starting point for scrum masters who are not inherently empathetic (count me in). Listening empathically to what your team members say and recognizing what you perceive and hear

for example, Elena, you seem to be concerned. How can I assist you?

I understand you are worried about Matt's actions, David. What do you want to happen?

They understand when you offer them your empathetic ears. They feel protected and at ease enough to reveal much more. The scrum master creates connections, heals team members, obtains trust, and achieves influence via empathy.

Being Ethical: The Scrum Master's moral compass must be strong. Being ethical refers to how a servant leader takes decisions, disciplines himself or herself, and selects the correct thing to do for the team. The Scrum Master may also urge the team to self-reflect and set high moral and ethical standards.

Team members continually notice and connect to the moral foundation of the servant leader's behaviors and corporate objectives.

If you have entrenched ethics and professionalism in yourself as a scrum master, you will be able to deliver them to the team.

The Scrum Master may see that the team has to develop and that they must be empowered and trained to conduct their own meetings, hold each other responsible, interact with users and POs, and produce value. And if the Scrum Master determines that he or she is not giving the most value to the team, they should either step down or move on.

Chapter 6: Making the scrum Transition

While there are numerous reasons that have already been discussed, this could be the tipping point in your career.

If you decide to transfer your team to the Scrum framework, bear in mind that it will not be without its challenges. This chapter will look at several of the most frequent transitional challenges and offer the simplest approaches to preventing them.

Team members that are resistant to change include: When it comes to the problems that are typically encountered while transitioning to Scrum, probably the most aggravating for a potential Scrum master is the team's hidden, overt, passive, and aggressive opposition. While the best way to deal with this resistance will likely differ from team to team, knowing what to look for will help you nip it in the bud as soon as possible.

For starters, active opposition is the easiest to recognize since it is frequently restricted to a small group of jaded and cranky people who don't like anything that comes in their way of doing things. However, if this issue is not addressed on a one-on-one, personal level, these agitators may generate a galvanizing message that spreads to other team members until there is an active block to prevent the change from occurring.

This is usually accompanied by overt opposition, in which individuals opposed to the change publicly badmouth the process and attempt to persuade even more team members out of participating. The sole advantage of overt opposition is that it is simple to tell who is doing what, allowing you to get to the bottom of the situation. When dealing with these individuals, it is critical to do so in such a way that you turn foes into friends rather than doing something that could further harm morale.

Unfortunately, overt resistance is not nearly as common as passive resistance, which is far more difficult to identify and, as a result, far more harmful to the cause. While they may learn what to do, they will only ever do the bare minimum of testing required to get by, rather than embracing the process to the extent that the process as a whole is likely to improve. This is an even bigger problem since it may lead to faults not being detected and other team members having to spend time covering for the one who is resisting.

The most difficult aspect of dealing with resistance is that it may be a subconscious reaction in a team member who looks to have entirely bought into the process at first sight. Remember that just because a team member knows Scrum is the correct thing to do does not imply it is the simplest thing to do, which is where the mental disconnect may occur.

To break past this mental barrier, the objective should be to instill in the company the notion that this kind of change is unavoidable. If team members think that Scrum is already a done deal, they will be less inclined to dispute it and more likely to learn how to make the change as simple to manage as feasible.

Motivation is also vital in this case since it is necessary to instill a sense of urgency in the change. Selling Scrum as a method of assisting a failing organization, whether this is the reality or not, may be a powerful way of swiftly dispelling uncertainty.

Misinterpretation of the procedure: Because the Scrum process is so different from many of its alternatives, team members can easily become confused, despite their best intentions. In reality, it is fairly usual for team members to believe they understand Scrum only to discover that they are confusing a number of separate, comparable procedures.

To help them get in the correct mindset, the team must first grasp that what is happening is a significant cultural shift for the organization that will affect how every member of the team spends at least a chunk of their day. One of the most prevalent misconceptions is the distinction between deadlines and estimates, which are extremely different and may take some getting used to. It is critical to remember that genuine reeducation is learning to conceive of production as a process, which includes learning to think in increments and managing expectations in a new way.

Meetings: Depending on how the workplace was previously organized, adjusting to the notion of a cross-functional team where everyone under-stands the project might be difficult. If a tight meeting policy is not enforced early on, you will discover that employees continue to attend far too many meetings each day, and the team's productivity suffers as a consequence.

To adequately address these difficulties, it is critical that the team make a complete shift to Scrum at once, since going slowly would only exacerbate matters. At the same time, it is critical to recognize that the team will likely need some time to adjust to the absence of top-down management, and you will need to provide assistance during this period as well.

Factor of intimidation: When teams begin to manage their own work, each member will naturally have much more responsibility for decision-making, prioritizing, and scheduling, which can feel like a lot of extra pressure. To alleviate this worry, make it obvious that virtually all of these choices will be taken by the team as a whole. Another method to make this aspect of the process seem more doable is to begin with smaller teams right away. This will reduce the number of moving parts to a minimum, making the whole procedure seem less scary right from the start. If you have a bigger team and are beginning with smaller teams to make the process more manageable, it is critical that they stay as cross-functional as feasible.

Chapter 7: Success Strategies

make a point of not planning ahead of time. Many teams, particularly those just starting out with Scrum, nevertheless feel the need to

Before they begin, they should plan anything. This might result in what is known as analysis paralysis. This happens when the planning step of any specific project often grinds work on that aim to a standstill as buy-in is acquired from several sources over a period of days, if not weeks. Remember, Scrum was supposed to be an adaptive framework for inspection, which means that it is contradictory to have numerous team members waiting for a single employee to complete prepping so they can go to work.

It is critical to remember that in order for Scrum to be utilized successfully, users must value the act of creation and, with it, the inherent risk of failure, not simply the documentation of the process. It also prioritizes the individual ties that guarantee people work successfully together rather than mindlessly obeying a set of rules. This means that, while there is no harm in a specific individual doing some early legwork on a project before bringing in the entire team, the point at which this becomes a disadvantage is when waiting for this one person prevents a larger number of individuals from generating any real type of value for an extended period of time.

While finding the right mix of pre-production and production can be difficult at first because you don't know what you're looking for from your team, it will become easier with practice. A decent rule of thumb is that if it takes more than two days to completely prepare for the start of a new project, your team may be experiencing analysis paralysis.

Rather than spending time planning everything ahead of time, teams may just get started and utilize the opportunity for feedback given at the Sprint Review to alter processes as required. This may also be extended to the development of the product backlog. Furthermore, instead of being arbitrarily assigned, the product owner could emerge empirically from the available stock of stakeholders.

While you and your team may initially find it difficult to begin a sprint without first completing a product backlog, it is entirely possible, assuming, of course, that the team already has a general idea of what is required in the business in question and a project or project charter to work from.

Using this information, your team should be able to generate a reasonable idea of what their first sprint should entail before getting started. Remember that the essential words here are starting. The aim of this first sprint is to create something that can be demoed and perhaps even delivered.

While this occasionally results in things that are completely wrong or otherwise unshippable, the goal isn't to get everything right away but rather to get everyone working through the inspect and adapt cycle as quickly as possible. This, in turn, will require genuine stakeholders to attend the demo at the conclusion of the first sprint in order for you to judge its success.

Don't be concerned about advanced tools: It is usual for new teams to put off beginning the Sprint process while they research the many tools available to assist them in making Scrum as simple and straightforward to use as feasible. While there is nothing wrong with looking for a good Scrum assistance tool, it is important to wait until you have a clear idea of which aspects of the Scrum process require electronic assistance.

The motivation is clear, particularly among teams that currently work for technology corporations. After all, why wouldn't you utilize technology to fix this and all of your other problems? In practice, however, Scrum's electronic tools are often more difficult to use than their analog counterparts. This happens for a variety of reasons, which may be broadly classified into three groups. For starters, they make it more difficult to openly exchange information. Second, they may make the information that is successfully communicated via them less apparent while also making the information that is made accessible to interested parties more slowly.

Looking at expensive tools so early in the process is like putting the wagon before the horse; it is more vital to get started than it is to get started perfectly with the ideal equipment. Being too concerned with a certain tool set is a simple way to put off beginning to adopt the Scrum method while still feeling productive.

Don't fall into this trap; instead, start with what you have and build your way up from there.

When you initially start utilizing the Scrum approach, you should find that a basic pen and paper tracking system readily meets all of your tracking requirements. This will allow you to get started fast and effortlessly and to begin your first Sprint without first confirming that everything is exactly right. Furthermore, most of the time, the simplest and most effective way of consistently improving communication within your team is to simply ensure that everyone working on a given project is physically located near one another.

You should also make sure that the room includes lots of whiteboards or other writing surfaces and that everyone is facing the center rather than being separated into their own tiny zones. Finally, you'll want to make sure that the group is isolated from the rest of the organization so that they have some privacy.

Maintain Product Owner Involvement: A typical issue that many sprints confront over time is a product owner who is excited and ready to participate at the start of the sprint but then drops off when it comes time to transform ideas into reality. A product owner is as much a member of a sprint team as anybody else, so they should ideally be present at every daily scrum, as well as the sprint planning meeting and the sprint retrospective and review. The product owner must also be present during work hours to give insight to team members who have queries. When the product owner is not actively dealing with shareholders, they should participate in the sprint process.

Remember that the Scrum Team model was designed to be as advantageous to productivity, creativity, and flexibility as possible, but it can only do so if the Product Owner is as devoted to respect, openness, focus, bravery, and dedication as the rest of the team. The sole exception is if your team adheres to the most stringent and current interpretation of Scrum, which restricts the Daily Scrum to the development team alone. However, there is still the option for others to observe the meeting, which should include both the product owner and the scrum master.

While it may be difficult to tell if your product owner is putting in enough time and effort early in your team's Sprint experience, you will be able to tell if they added enough input by how they respond to your Sprint Review. If the product owner utilizes the review time to offer comments on the findings, you know they weren't engaged enough in the process. Instead, an engaged product owner will lead the conversation with stakeholders, users, or customers during the sprint review.

While the product owner should be as accessible as possible, there are numerous scenarios in which they may need to legitimately be absent from the process for an extended period of time. The first is when they are engaging with shareholders; in most situations, these sorts of meetings should be planned apart from Sprint-based obligations. In any case, the product owner should leave a surrogate in place to offer their feedback based on the information that is currently readily accessible.

Avoid Using Stretch Goals: Stretch goals have long been used in various contexts to lay out extra targets that may be realized if specific circumstances are satisfied. They are, however, antagonistic to the sprint technique and should never be utilized during a sprint for any reason.

Stretch objectives may come in two varieties; it is critical that you be aware of both and where they originate from so that the Scrum Master can guarantee they do not detract from the good team-centric mindset that the Sprint is creating. The stretch goal offered by someone outside of the team is the worst form of stretch goal and may frequently seem to damage group unity.

Stretch objectives with a set scope and date are the most challenging for Scrum teams to work through because they demand the team to start with a deadline and then work backwards to identify how to fulfill it, which is essentially the reverse of how things typically happen. Worse, when objections are raised, they are usually met with a reaffirmation to "get it done" or by simply adding more people to the team, which does nothing to improve the situation if the new people don't know anything about Scrum.

Otherwise, stretch goals have been known to appear on occasion when team members attempt to determine what the development team is capable of, despite the development team's objections. It is critical to remember that the development team will have the greatest understanding of what it can do given different external constraints, and spending time fighting with them is just wasting time that may be spent elsewhere.

The answer to this frequent problem is quite simple: let the team assess how much work it can actually do within the constraints of the sprint. This is not to say that the first evaluation of what will be done is fixed in stone, but it does imply that no member of the team should ever feel forced to commit to more work than they believe they can reasonably do. Forcing a team to agree to stretch objectives would almost certainly breed mistrust among team members if the stretch goals were not accomplished effectively. Distrust may rise to resentment, and both will result in lesser-quality work being performed repeatedly.

After all, if the stretch goal failed, there must have been a reason. Therefore, do your team a favor and avoid stretch goals and the witch hunts that they will inevitably spawn.

Make it clear that no personal sacrifice is required. When your team is in the middle of a sprint, they will frequently be forced to solve complex problems on the fly. There is, however, a correct and wrong approach to addressing these challenges, and the distinction between the two might be hazy without the proper context.

First and foremost, it is important to recognize that by coming together and tackling these types of difficulties, the team organically develops, which not only makes the unit as a whole better prepared for the future but also more cohesive as a team. As a result, although it is terrific if one person cracks the nut that the whole team was working on, if that individual goes to near-superhuman lengths to do it, the team learns an entirely different lesson.

Rather than learning to handle challenges collaboratively, the team in this scenario learns to depend on the individual they know will always come through in a pinch. Worse, this person may begin to wield excessive power over the team as a whole, which means they may end up assigning mandates and even setting stretch goals without even realizing it. They may also pose a variety of additional concerns for the team, such as blocking other members from acquiring the capacity to creatively explore and solve problems.

If one person constantly knows all of the answers, they deprive others of knowing why specific answers exist, which damages the team as a whole. If this continues unchecked for an extended length of time, it is also probable that some members of the team may get disinterested in the process as a whole since it will rapidly become clear that depending on the star is inconsistent with standard Scrum norms. Ultimately, this will demolish the team idea at its core, and nothing will be done, even if the star is still trying everything in their power to shine.

The simplest approach to preventing this sort of problem is to catch it early in the Sprint planning process. As long as things are correctly planned from the start, there should be no need for anybody to go above and beyond to get things done.

Additionally, if this type of scenario occurs on a regular basis, you may find it beneficial to pad out your sprint times in order to prevent things from devolving into the need for such feats in the way they previously have.

Chapter 8: Stories from the Trenches

Terminales Portuarios Peruanos:

This is a firm centered on port and marine services. Their IT department creates software for its own internal operations and methods. Traditionally, it had followed a set release schedule that was progressively failing to meet the objectives it required. The aim for a team of 50 people was to provide a new product at the conclusion of each cycle, but the process wasn't iterative, and the teams were constantly held up towards the end of development, making it impossible to reach their goals. The capacity of the IT organization to deploy new software every 30 days the organization opted to expand Scrum by reducing and eliminating cross-team dependencies and integration concerns while increasing transparency.

In 2017, the firm faced a future deadline that it knew it had to achieve, so it formed a Scrum team to guarantee the date was completed without incident. Their first step of implementation began with bringing stakeholders together to match corporate goals with user demands before aligning the outcomes with the product backlog. The product owner collaborated with the teams to arrange and optimize the product backlog using impact mapping and story mapping. The product owner and the teams collaborated to create integrated software.

The firm transitioned from a typical project management approach that valued schedule management and activity monitoring to a methodology that prioritized product delivery and daily progress. The initial release was made available within one month, and the product was fully operational within three months. The old methodology would have resulted in the first release in three months.

Vodafone: Vodafone, one of the world's leading mobile communication carriers, operates in more than 30 countries and collaborates with approximately 50 other providers. Vodafone Turkey, one of these partners, has more than 20 million users, yet the Turkish telecoms business is tremendously competitive, and they required assistance managing the severe time-to-market pressure they were experiencing.

Overall, three situations needed to be addressed in order to alleviate the pressure on the demand for increased productivity. The first was time-to-market pressure, but there were also higher business expectations, an excessively extended time-to-market timeframe, and a communication gap between all members of the team. While the first problem could only be solved by improving the second and third, Scrum had solutions for all three.

The extended amount of time between when a product was produced and brought to market was caused by the fact that testers and developers were seen as distinct entities rather than as part of a single development team. As a consequence, the latency between the two handoffs was substantial, and its overall responsiveness suffered. Similarly, the old system's communication gap was filled by the enhanced openness of the Scrum Framework and the realization that everyone is working toward the same sprint goal at the same time.

To address these difficulties, the firm established a Scrum team inside the IT department with the aim of reducing turnaround time while also improving overall product quality. Several sprints were completed with this new Scrum team as part of this pilot program, and the progress of each was tracked. Because of the increased efficiency provided by the Scrum methodology, the pilot team was able to triple its total productivity in only three months.

With such excellent results, the firm chose to scale the Scrum methodology across the organization.

After around five months of adjusting to the new way of doing things, the firm reported that Scrum teams were functioning at double the efficiency of the previous model across the board. Furthermore, the company noticed a significant decrease in customer complaints as well as reported defects.

SoftwarePeople: In 2004, a Danish business called SoftwarePeople joined with a Bangladeshi investment group and made the choice to establish a new subsidiary company in Bangladesh immediately. The company then employed 20 individuals in a single week and began employing standard procedures in both locations, with the ultimate objective of obtaining CMMI Level 3 certification in around 18 months. This resulted in endless pit stops and roadblocks until the team returned to Scrum in an attempt to improve communication. As a consequence, long-running projects were canceled, integration and technical challenges were resolved, and smaller work batches were implemented, resulting in enhanced integration at all levels and significantly quicker delivery of demonstrable commercial value.

It all began in 2006, when the organization was seeking a method to move away from their failing CMMI process. Someone in the firm had heard of Scrum, and everyone thought it sounded fascinating, so the CTO and three of the project managers decided to give it a try and enrolled in a Scrum Master training course.

That same month, the CEOs of both countries met in the UK for product owner training to ensure they all understood what made Scrum unique.

When a particularly complex project appeared on the horizon, they began experimenting with Scrum in the Danish office. The Scrum team not only completed the project successfully, but their results were so compelling that they persuaded the corporation to implement the methodology across both locations.

Their implementation strategy began with Scrum teams working on customer and research and development projects to establish a consistent rhythm. The approach would then be extended to worldwide teams, who would be able to collaborate more readily as a result of the added knowledge Scrum brought to the project. They noticed great results across the board after a series of sprints, including a 100 percent boost in efficiency in certain situations. While some team members still had questions, everyone had a much better understanding of their responsibilities and the tools they had to ensure they met their objectives.

Conclusion

Thank you for reading Scrum: The Complete Step-By-Step Guide to Managing Product Development Using the Agile Framework. We hope it was educational and provided you with all of the tools you need to reach your objectives.

Just because you've read this book doesn't imply there's nothing more to learn about the subject, and broadening your horizons is the only way to achieve mastery.

The Scrum framework has something for almost every sort of company, but it is crucial to remember that even the most basic of benefits take time to observe. As a consequence, if you are ready to be the Scrum champion at your firm, it is critical that you recognize that it will take some time before you see results since getting a Scrum team to operate well together is all about training and practice. Despite the short-term productivity impact, the ultimate outcome will be significantly more effective, which is why, despite the needed training, it remains a great value offer. Remember that transforming your team into a Scrum team is a marathon, not a sprint; therefore, slow and steady wins the race.

Finally, if you found this book beneficial in any way, please leave a review on Amazon!!